FLAT
AT THE
TOP

UNIQUE CHARACTERISTICS OF THE PLATEAU, PRAIRIE AND MESA

Geography Book Grade 4 | Children's Earth Sciences Books

First Edition, 2020

Published in the United States by Speedy Publishing LLC, 40 E Main Street, Newark, Delaware 19711 USA.

© 2020 Baby Professor Books, an imprint of Speedy Publishing LLC

Baby Professor Books are available at special discounts when purchased in bulk for industrial and sales-promotional use. For details contact our Special Sales Team at Speedy Publishing LLC, 40 E Main Street, Newark, Delaware 19711 USA. Telephone (888) 248-4521 Fax: (210) 519-4043. www.speedybookstore.com

10 9 8 7 6 * 5 4 3 2 1

Print Edition: 9781541977730
Digital Edition: 9781541977877

See the world in pictures. Build your knowledge in style.
www.speedypublishing.com

TABLE OF CONTENTS

The Earth is a truly remarkable place. Although most of our planet is made up of more water than land, the land consists of many different and interesting formations. Land formations can be defined as areas of land that have features that are different than other areas.

Three land formations will be the focus of this book. They are the prairies, plateaus and mesas. Read facts of each of these land formations and how they affect local ecosystems. Let's get started!

Detailed image of Earth
showing North and South
America

A PRAIRIE

A prairie is a section of land that is both big and wide. It can stretch for miles and miles. Although it is mostly flat and even, it can contain some areas which have rolling hills. Nonetheless, the hills are so short that they are called pimples.

A Prairie land

Panorama of the prairie and mountains near Boulder, Colorado

There are prairies in the United States. In fact, most of the land between the Rocky Mountains and the Mississippi River consists of prairies.

Because a lot of grass grows on prairies, they are often referred to as grasslands. Prairie grass does not look like the grass that is carefully mown and manicured on a person's lawn.

Prairie grass

If you look at a prairie, you will notice tall, wavy grass blowing in the wind. The roots of the grass, which have a long lifespan, can extend to deep areas under the ground to access water. Because the grass helps to keep the soil from washing away, there is almost no erosion.

Prairie grass keeps the soil from erosion.

The soil on the land of a prairie is very fertile. Weather conditions are generally moderate. These conditions result in areas where crops can grow.

Prairie town of Cowley and Pincher Creek, Alberta, Canada

A lot of grains, such as wheat, oats, and rye, for example, grow in prairies in North America. Corn can also be grown.

Corn field in North Dakota

This is one of the reasons why many settlers moved west in the nineteenth century. There was so much opportunity to gain good land to farm.

The Westward Movement was influenced by the desire to gain good farm land.

14

When the settlers moved to the prairies in the Midwestern states, they noticed one creature and they called it the prairie dog.

Hunting of prairie dogs in New Mexico.

15

In fact, the creature is not a species of dog at all! The creature was given this name because the sounds it made were the sounds that reminded the settlers of the sounds that dogs made.

An adult Black-Tailed prairie dog and its pup

The prairie dog is a rodent and there are several different types. It is an omnivore, which means it eats both plants and animals. Its most common source of food are seeds and plant life.

A family of prairie dog eating grass

Prairie dogs usually grow to a height of about twelve inches and they like to burrow. Burrowing is when an animal digs a tunnel or hole in the ground. The soft earth of the prairie is an ideal place for the prairie dog to burrow.

Prairie dogs live in underground burrows.

PRAIRIE ECOSYSTEMS

An ecosystem describes the various interactions of different organisms and their surrounding environment.

Prairie Nature Preserve, Cook County, Illinois

21

Prairie dogs are especially important to the ecosystem of prairies as they are a keystone species. This means that they provide homes for more than one hundred and fifty other species of animals.

Prairie dogs are vital in the survival of other animals in the prairie.

Prairie dogs provide homes for other species of animals in the prairie ecosystem.

Prairie dogs provide these homes through their many networks of tunnels that they burrow in the soft soil the prairies provide. They create many different tunnels for various purposes from sleeping to storage to connecting with other prairie dogs.

These tunnels can later be repurposed by snakes, mice, insects and various other creatures.

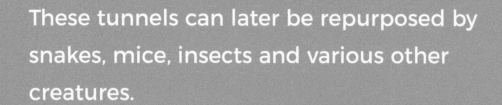

Mice find shelter in the burrows prairie dogs create.

24

Since so many animals can find homes thanks to the prairie dog, it also encourages predators.

Group of prairie dogs

Eagles prey on prairie dogs.

Prairie dogs hide from eagles and cayotes, for example. The relation between predator and prey can be demonstrated in a food chain.

Food chains are another important part of the ecosystem. Since animals can eat multiple different things, multiple food chains can be combined to make a food web. A food web is more accurate and helps show the delicate balance to maintain the ecosystem.

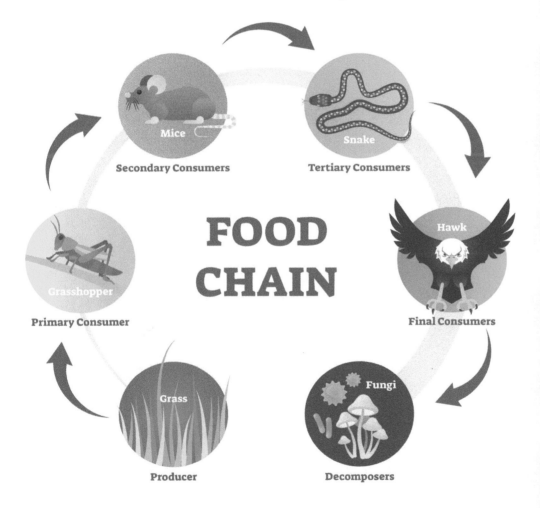

Too much hunting will mean not enough food for other species, which can have a ripple effect. Since the prairie dog is a keystone species, removing it from the prairie would devastate the ecosystem, and change it drastically.

Hunters hunting prairie dog

As a result, ecosystems are not only about food chains, but also about land, because without the soft soil prairies offer, prairie dogs would not be able to have such an impact. It is the land that provides the most basic source of food and shelter.

Prairie dogs are able to burrow their holes because of the soft prairie soil.

A PLATEAU

Plateau is a word which comes from French. It means "table land." The word describes a section of land that is elevated above the land around it on at least one side. Unlike hills or mountains, plateaus are typically flat.

High plateau of the Cockburn Range, El Questro Station, Kimberley, Australia

However, there are many different types, and, like mountains, they are associated with tectonic plates. Tectonic plates refer to rock on which the land and oceans rest. Tectonic plates can move, shift and rub together.

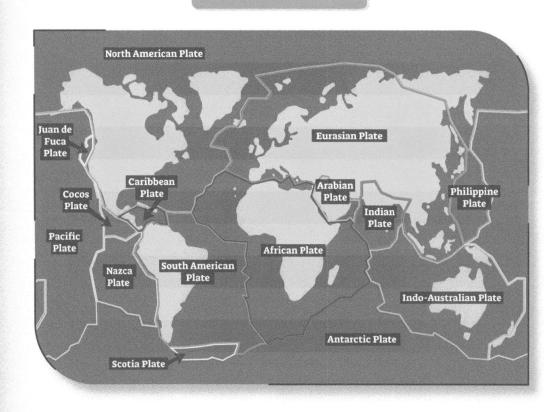

TECTONIC PLATES

North American Plate

Juan de Fuca Plate

Eurasian Plate

Cocos Plate

Caribbean Plate

Arabian Plate

Philippine Plate

Indian Plate

Pacific Plate

African Plate

Nazca Plate

South American Plate

Indo-Australian Plate

Antarctic Plate

Scotia Plate

This movement can cause earthquakes. In addition, tectonic plates can collide. They can move together and slide upwards or downwards. This can lead to large mountains.

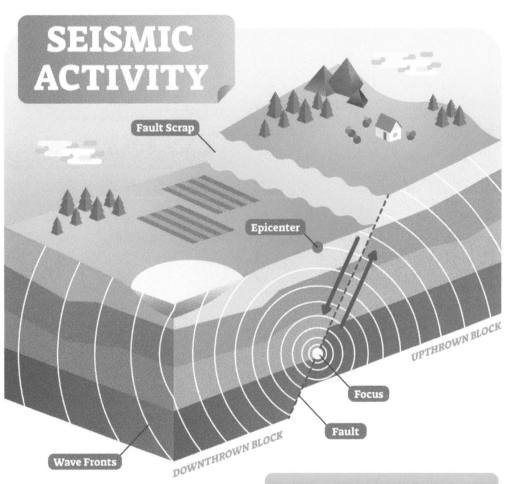

SEISMIC ACTIVITY

Fault Scrap

Epicenter

UPTHROWN BLOCK

Focus

Fault

DOWNTHROWN BLOCK

Wave Fronts

A diagram of two tectonic plates moving against each other.

Where plateaus are found near mountain ranges, they are thought to be created as a result of the tectonic plates shifting upward.

Large dry mountain plateau, Gros Morne National Park, Newfoundland, Canada

As the tectonic plates lift upwards, they form a flat, raised, portion of land. This type of a plateau is called an intermontane plateau.

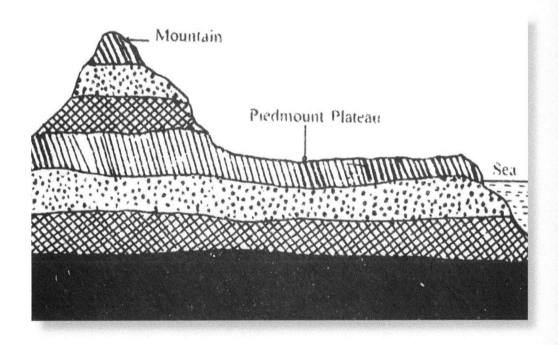

Mountain

Piedmount Plateau

Sea

INTERMONTANE PLATEAU

Some of the largest plateaus on Earth, such as the Tibetan Plateau, in Asia, or the Altiplanto in South America are believed to have been formed this way. They are about 15,000 to 12,000 feet, respectively.

Tibetan Plateau

Bolivian Altiplano

Another way plateaus can form around mountainous areas is through volcanic activity. Volcanic plateaus are formed when lava flows accumulate, or gather, and harden.

Volcanic activity can also result in the formation of plateaus.

Over many millions of years, these eruptions of lava and basalt build up to form large plateaus. Volcanic plateaus can be noted for having a lot of basalt. As a result, they can sometimes be called basalt plateaus.

Plateau basalt along the southern coast of Scoresby Sund, East Greenland

There is also a type of plateau called a continental plateau. Geologists, people who study land, do not agree on exactly how these types of land formations come to be. These types of plateaus are raised up very slowly.

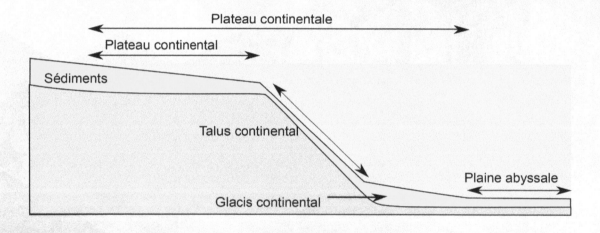

A diagram of a plateau continental

A feature of the continental plateau is the presence of canyons. Since a continental plateau forms slowly, it is possible for rivers and streams to erode great canyons into them.

An illustration of a continental landform with a plateau and canyon.

The Colorado Plateau, for example, is where the Grand Canyon is located. The Grand Canyon is called a gorge as it is very narrow but has walls that stretch up to a mile high. The steep drop with flat lands all around it shows the presence of plateaus.

Colorado Plateau

43

Most plateaus have some level of erosion along the edges. However, some plateaus, like the Colorado Plateau, which have such deep levels of erosion are called dissected plateaus.

This is because they have been cut into pieces or dissected. The erosion along plateaus is simply called dissection.

Dissections of the Colorado Plateau

45

MESAS AND
BUTTES

A mesa is like a plateau except for the fact that it is found on a mountain or a hill. Unlike a plateau, which only requires a steep, rocky slope on one side, a mesa is flat on top, but steep all around.

Mesa in Monument Valley, Arizona

Its shape is like that of a hill that has had its round top cut off. It can help to imagine a mesa as being a hill that is so flat giants could use it as a table. In fact, mesa is the Spanish word for table!

While a plateau has only one steep side, a mesa is steep all around - like a table.

Mesas, like canyons, are believed to have been formed by erosion from water that left behind only steep, hard rock. Over time, more and more erosion happens which wears down the sides of the mesa.

Black Mesa in New Mexico

This can turn a mesa into a butte, which is pronounced like the beginning of the word beautiful. A butte is just a mesa that is taller than it is wide.

Merrick's Butte, Monument Valley, Arizona

The top of the butte is made of hard rock which is harder to erode. This is why the height rarely changes, but buttes will, in time, become quite thin. Eventually, of course, even the caprock, the hard rock on top, will come to erode.

Camel Butte, Monument Valley, Arizona

Talus field below Devils Tower butte in Wyoming

When this happens, rocks and stones can fall from the top down the sides. These falling rocks are called talus or scree.

Buttes are also known to be found in very dry areas where it is hard for plant life to grow. Since erosion is critical for the formation of buttes, it makes sense that they would be found in arid or dry places.

The Pueblo of the Acoma people, New Mexico

The reason is that sandstone is soft and easy to break down. In seemingly desolate locations, buttes can often be the only major land formation around. Buttes are best known to be found in the south of the United States and Mexico.

Fajada butte, Colorado

55

Mesa Navajo Tribal majesty place, Monument Valley, Arizona, USA

56

Some very well-known buttes are in Monument Valley Navajo Tribal Park. These buttes are called *The Mittens* since they look just like mittens even down to the shape of the thumb!

Monument Valley is quite well known for all its strange land formations. A lot of the western movie genre has been filmed in Monument Valley because it is so well-known for its beautiful landscapes.

Monument Valley, Arizona

THE MESA VERDE NATIONAL PARK

Cliff dwellings in Mesa Verde National Parks, Colorado

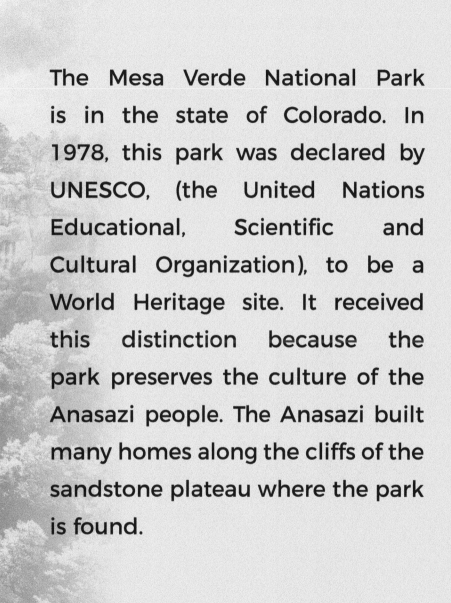

The Mesa Verde National Park is in the state of Colorado. In 1978, this park was declared by UNESCO, (the United Nations Educational, Scientific and Cultural Organization), to be a World Heritage site. It received this distinction because the park preserves the culture of the Anasazi people. The Anasazi built many homes along the cliffs of the sandstone plateau where the park is found.

The plateau has been dissected by streams to create many canyons and many mesas. The various places in the sandstone that was carved out by the water served the Anasazi well as they used these natural formations to build places to live.

Puye Cliff dwellings are runes where the ancient pueblo people, called Anasazi, lived.

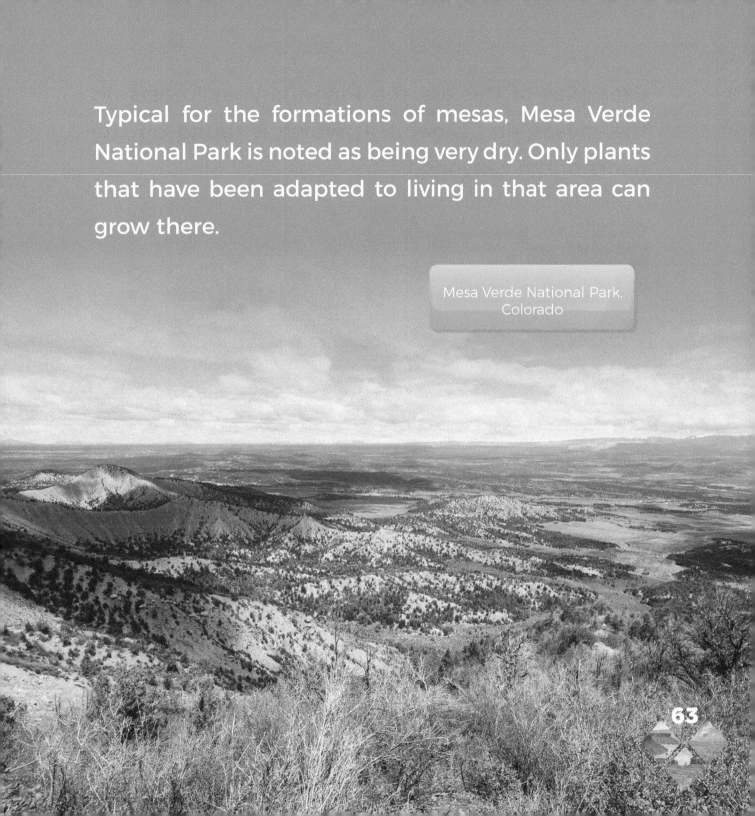

Typical for the formations of mesas, Mesa Verde National Park is noted as being very dry. Only plants that have been adapted to living in that area can grow there.

Mesa Verde National Park, Colorado

63

Examples of this are the Piñon-juniper forests on the mesas, and sagebrush which is found on the floors of the canyons.

Pinyon-juniper forest mixed with shrubs, cacti, and sage

64

There are also some animals that live in the Park. Elks are the most populous, but there are also bears, lions, and some small mammals as well. Reptiles such as snakes and lizards are also quite common.

Elks live in the Mesa Verde National Park.

65

While different from prairies, these areas boast their own unique and adapted ecosystem.

An panorama of the lush forests of the Mesa Verde National Park.

As you can see the Earth is a very marvelous, complex, and beautiful place. Mesas, prairies, and plateaus are not only formed over millions of years by their surroundings, but they also affect the ecosystems around them.

The interactions between land formations and animals is so complex, we are only just beginning to understand how delicate the balance is.

Land formation and animals affect the ecosystem

Every organism is connected in complex ways, and this even goes all the way back to simply where they live. Is it dry and full of sandstone? Are their mesas or plateaus? Is the land fertile like a prairie? Is there plenty of food and water?

Roan Antilope and zebra at Nyika plateau, Malawi, Africa

What about where you live? Is it rocky or fertile? Does it affect how you live and the jobs that are available? Imagine that so many parts of your life can come back to the formations of land around you!

Visit

BABY PROFESSOR

EDUCATION KIDS

www.speedypublishing.com
to download Free Baby Professor eBooks
and view our catalog of new and exciting
Children's Books

Lightning Source UK Ltd.
Milton Keynes UK
UKHW051327040121
376379UK00002B/60